6 Months In a Van

My Life On The American Road

By Martin Goldberg

Dedication

To all those "lazy" millennials, who sacrifice today to prosper tomorrow.

Table of Contents

1. Introduction: The Abbreviated Life

"You WANT to be homeless?" The words fell sharply from her mouth, second only to an incredulous color at the eyes. She drew an arm to her hip and pinched several fingers into the skin-tight grip of her shirt fabric. *This has got to be a very bad joke*, you could almost hear her say, like the thought bubble of an irate Marvel character, pre-Disney of course. It felt like April Fools, even though that date was still several months way from being reborn.

To be fair, my friend had a point. Speaking from the perspective of social hierarchy, my plans were ridiculous. I had good income, a degree from a respected school, and no significant debt. Why on earth would I then elect to forgo having a permanent apartment or house in favor the sweaty and ignominious life of a mobile pack rat unit, forever done and condemned to the social circle of a misanthropic chigger? Was I determined to write a novel?

On that latter point, I suppose you could send me up to the river, but the truth is rather wilder. I decided to embark on this project because it spoke to a profound value that has powered my life and objectives: maximum freedom. We live in a society which pushes the idea on people at every turn, but the applied reality is a lot less common. At every turn, people are sanctioned, taxed, and punished for trying to observe even a basic degree of individuality in their own lives. Even fundamental actions like building something on property you own is heavily regulated all the way to K Street's red light district. Try to defy these dictums and you are heading for massive fines, if not also incarceration.

In the context of a regular living space, you don't fare much better. Apartment offices will tax the Starfish Tuna out of you at every turn, and then up the rates unexpectedly. All of this while trying to punish you for the behavior of neighbors. For instance, I was once threatened with eviction for simply walking around in my apartment, which apparently bothered the person downstairs. Never mind that they were loud and boisterous in general, including throwing parties that lasted until 3am; just shut up and pay for the privilege.

Home ownership is pushed as an alternative, rather nebulous argument supporting freedom. After all, you become your own boss, with a space that is technically all yours to inhabit and play with. Maybe throw in the adoring wife and 1.75 kids for good measure. Only problem is, you don't actually own the place. You can buy the house and pay off your mortgage, which usually includes a double payment of principal and interest, but it fails to end there. Now as an "independent homeowner" you must still pay for property taxes, HOA fees, and upkeep/utilities. If you fail to pay for the first two in particular, you will quickly lose your house to the government. So you essentially pay for a low-cost rental once the initial charges have been banished from your forever alone bank account.

Looking at and experiencing some of these options led me to believe that I had nothing to lose by trying something else. After all, the 2008 financial crisis and its ensuing offspring economy presented a troubling reality to the Millennial and Generation Z complements: one in which the classic stability enjoyed by their Boomer forerunners was no longer guaranteed. Senior employees found themselves unemployed, life savings turned into spent lottery tickets, and retirement plans went up in smoke. The "Do thirty and collect a pension" mindset was gone, replaced by uneasy and barebones benefit structures, along with the expanded popularity of the 1099 (Independent Contractor) job type. The world was made anew.

In response to these dire waves of unmaking, young people began looking for ways to cut back on the costs of subsistence. While some of those expenses might be fixed, the level and frequency at which they occur stands to drastically affect your future, potentially making or busting its viability. We already know how pricy housing can be, so many adventurous folks turned in the direction of vehicle living as an alternative to reduce their overhead (derp) and improve other quality of life aspects.

I had known about the concept for some years prior to taking the plunge, but it always seemed held off and unworkable when compared with the "normal" life I had been accustomed to since time immemorial. "How will I stay clean?" I would wonder openly. "Where can I store food?" And most importantly, if only on a private level, "What will others think?" I wrestled, or rather cat-fought, with these issues, because the idea never seemed realistic enough to be properly implemented. The crowning justification my mind presented was this flippant and arrogant offering: "I'm better than that. It's only an option for people who can't afford real housing."

About a year later, as I was sitting in traffic on the long commute for my new job, the thought hit me: *You are wasting your life.* My immediate reaction was to dispel the notion. *I'm making good money, so it's not a problem.* But it was, and like it or not, my brain had a good point. I was spending almost 4 hours a day locked in the severely manic depressive coffin of a Ford sedan, limited in what I could accomplish during that time. My car's CD player had gone out earlier, and with no aux input hookup the prospect of audiobook listening was fairly grim. So it was music and boredom. Click, click, repeat. Four hours a day, five days a week, roughly 1040 hours a year of my life going to the garbage disposal, and I couldn't even use it for sleep. Whenever I got home, much of my downtime was spent doing exactly that to absorb the exhaustion of my commuting and work schedule, leaving me with about 3-4 hours to my lonesome out of 24, or less than 20 percent in that timeframe. And even on the weekends I usually suffered from the after effects, leaving little time for dance or errors if I wanted to make progress in my own world.

This "Abbreviated Life," amid which every action and waking hour seems to unquestionably relate to or revolve around your job, always struck me as immensely unappealing. We are more interesting than our employment titles, at least in my glorious opinion. When you allow yourself to become so lovingly tethered to the clockwork chains of a profession, it's easy to lose part of the human experience that is life in return for garnering some quick cash.

As a result of these calculations, I concluded that spending more downtime in my vehicle would majorly enhance the quality of life I enjoyed on several different fronts. So around the holiday season I began carefully cultivating a planned resolution for the next year: to be independent and free as a Mobile Goldberg. The following is my story of how it worked out, what I learned, and how the experience could potentially benefit you.

1. Finding a Car

If you ask the average person what they think living in a vehicle looks like, they'll probably give you a dismal face to begin with. That's because they're imagining being crammed into the back of a Toyota Corolla, trying desperately to keep their tushy balanced upon the oil-stained cloth seats, with their neck likely crushed up, Picasso style, against the armrest, where God knows what sort of precious substances have sunken into the leather. It's the living embodiment of being a gypsy drifter, or profane highway tomato. In short, stay away.

The reality is a little less depressing, as long as you possess an imagination. Within the broad spectrum of the autosphere lie several distinct categories of living, much like model types in real estate offering houses, townhomes, and condos. Your goal is to find an option that fits individual needs without compromising the cost-saving arguments at base level. If you are spending more to go mobile than renting/buying, stop and reassess. Minimalism should never bleed you worse than Normality.

A. RV Living

One of the initial categories, an idea which drips of Americanism, is to live out of a Recreational Vehicle. These lumbering behemoths offer comforts native to a house or apartment, but eliminate the stationary insecurities. You can up and leave at any time, but must carry possessions (and mortar discharge facilities) along for the ride. They come in traditional trailer models, lobsterback (mounted over pickup truck beds) versions, or the massive tour bus-sized Winnebago class. Most models provide you with a mobile toilet and storage tank, a shower, and some refrigeration unit. You can hookup at RV parks, and drain out the nasty on wheels at many municipal utility plants, sometimes for free. For certain people, the RV is also an option to retire on the cheap, with the goal of traveling much of the drivable world.

At the same time, RVs come with a slew of central downsides. To begin, they don't do so well on the fuel side, especially if you happen to have the all-in-one version with lots of space. Furthermore, the size and specificity of the model may render it unserviceable by regular mechanic shops, necessitating that you go to a special (and pricy) mobile home technician for repairs. Consider the gravity of this if the vehicle breaks down on the side of the highway; getting it towed will not be fun. You also become a lot more visible, which can be a plus or minus, depending on the area. Additional questions relate to the costs of RV park fees, and whether you are allowed to park in particular areas due to the vehicle's size.

B. Utility Van (Or Truck)

Depending on who you ask, there is some disagreement over what constitutes a van in this category because of model size differences. In the larger corner, a popular option is to buy a GMC Savana or Ford E-350 for the interior space. You can throw down a mattress in the back, install shelving or storage compartments on the side interior, and even relegate some acreage for a cooking area. Mounting a rod behind the front seats can allow for the installation of curtains, giving added privacy when you are parking or sleeping. There are even some Ford Transit vans which get modified for these purposes, representing the more petite category of vehicles.

The immediate benefit of the utility van modification lies in its interior room. Once you get out of the typical commuter vehicle categories, the absence of seat rows and clunky sidebar features on doors provides a much better environment to operate in and be yourself. Especially with the mattress size, you won't have to feel compressed, or otherwise "used," at least not while sleeping.

On the negative, you have some factors similar to the previous category. A utility truck/van does offer more space, but it also stands out starkly in the middle of the pack. Such vehicles are associated with tradesmen and repair companies, but they also draw unwanted attention should you choose to park at a library, or spend the night in some parking lot. This is less of an issue from a legal standpoint, but perception does matter. Any place where children frequent may become suspicious of a stereotypical "pedo van," and proceed to have authorities harass you. It might be the byproduct of ridiculous paranoia on the part of our modern culture, but the fact still stands for consideration.

Furthermore, utility vans have some downsides from a technical perspective. A Ford E-350 will clock in at 12-16 mpg, depending on the type of driving being done. The GMC Savana comes in not much better at 11-16 mpg. As for the Ford Transit, you're looking at a slightly better 15 mpg average, always dependent on the model. For all these options, driving traction in inclement weather can be limited depending on driver skill and the tires used, so take that into account if you live in a region that gets a lot of snow or ice.

C. SUV/Minivan Living

Arguably the most popular mobile home idea is to operate out of a regular consumer SUV or minivan. Such vehicles are widely available on the market and may feature lower gas or repair costs, but these come at the expense of space. Names that are frequently tossed around for the second category online include the Toyota Sienna, Honda Odyssey, and Chrysler Town and Country. I personally advise avoiding the latter like a UTI, but you will find some folks who seem happy enough with the performance. The minivan's biggest advantage rests with the length of the cargo area, far superior to smaller vehicles which might see you cramped if your height rises above the average range. Some of the newer models for these vans also feature AWD technology, a valuable touch depending on where you roam on the map. The year and brand can also affect whether seats are locked in, can be removed manually, or folded down using the "stow and go" benefit native to some parts of the market.

You might also like to go with the SUV route as an alternative. Sport Utility Vehicles shine in their unique way by providing a more comfy ride along with the critical space component. Some possibilities would be the Toyota Highlander, GMC Yukon, or Honda Element. The model you select will obviously influence how much room is available for use, and the general price tag of fueling it. Bigger options like the Yukon offer substantially roomier interiors, but the tradeoff is an atrocious mpg of 11-15, so you can expect that side of your expenses to go up. Larger models are also difficult to maneuver in narrow spaces, so they will not work for everyone. At the same time, small SUVs will give you lower gas costs at the expense of spacious operating quarters. Be especially careful to check the status of the rear seating; in the case of vehicles like the Highlander, they sometimes include an optional third row that you will need to modify if you intend on sleeping without becoming Cramps McGee.

In the case of a hybrid vehicle, be exceedingly careful with your purchase. Since much of the vehicle living community relies on lower cost options, it can be tempting to purchase a used SUV or other vehicle sporting the electric-gas fusion system. These machines are unquestionably beautiful, though they come with an ample risk relating to the hybrid battery. Replacing one of those suckers starts at $3,000, with labor generously dolloped on top. For this reason, you need to check the service history to see if that part has already been respawned. A hybrid vehicle over five years old with the factory battery and decent mileage is certainly cause for a bit of concern.

D. Sedan Living

Finally, we have the smaller category of folks who elect for traditionalism and attempt to live in a regular commuter car. The logic here can be as simple as availability, or the lower costs associated with a compact vehicle. A frequent one mentioned is the Toyota Prius, which promises very ideal fuel economy to keep your costs low. I have also heard people sing praises of the car's climate control system, which works off the hybrid battery with occasional support from the gas engine to maintain adequate temperature without the high power demands thrust on regular, gas-only vehicles. Providing you live in a state which is on the warmer side, such a feature can make nights a lot less sleepless, even if you are in Seattle.

The shortcomings of sedan living are fairly obvious. To begin, you have very limited space to utilize for the purposes of a bed. Few commuter cars have seats that will lay back all the way flat, so you can expect back pain or sore spots from attempting the venture, although it is possible to get used to the feeling. The particular design of individual chairs further limits HOW you can sleep, with many being uneven around the rotational hinge. One might attempt to sleep in the back row, but if you are on the taller side such a measure could quickly become uncomfortable. An exception might involve removing the backseat rest and extending oneself through the trunk; only problem is, in colder weather this will put you closer to the chill, unless some serious insulation is involved. Finally, sedans do not give you the level of privacy some folks will prefer when it comes to everyday changing or relaxation.

2. How I Chose a Vehicle

As I noted before, my previous vehicle was a 4-door sedan, so my experience with different models remained limited. I embarked on my search by scouting out used trucks with camper shells (which might serve as a dwelling) and SUVs in the same category. I found several Toyota Highlanders available, but they all suffered from the same problem: too old, high mileage, and still with the original hybrid battery. I wasn't about to snag something which would need a costly repair within its usage life because my goal was to maximize saving throughout the experience. For a while I wistfully considered the possibility of a Nissan or Dodge truck, probably as a result of ego more than common sense. I tossed in a Chrysler Town and Country van, largely because it included AWD, which was one factor I hoped to secure. In each case, the private sellers either refused, or were extremely evasive about giving me the VIN (Vehicle Identification Number). Here is one of the paramount rules of used car purchasing:

never in the name of sweet Jessica Alba's tushy should you buy something without running a VIN report. You have to make sure it's not stolen, and avoid any possibilities where the model was towed away from an accident and then patched up in a body shop. Few cars run the same after sustaining internal damage, no matter how pretty they are on the outside.

The reluctance of people I was dealing with led me to the classic dead water moment in car buying: you know roughly what you want for a specific price range, but it always seems to be elusive for your desperate, grimy hands. I quickly ruled out an RV, because the repair costs and maneuverability would be problematic in the area I was operating. From this junction I toyed with the idea of a Ford Ranger with a camper shell on the back, and further eyed the Chevy Blazer, which fit well in all ways except for its horrendous gas mileage. Since I had wandered into the neighborhood of star-gazing, I also considered the GMC Yukon, looking to heighten comfort space whilst still maintaining the fairly neutral look desired.

None of these guys struck me as especially endearing once they had been tested against the practical realities of what I would be doing on a day-to-day basis. As a result, my mind began wistfully drifting back to one of the first targets in my search: an early 1990s GMC Vandura, the quintessential camper van. I had found one at a dealer for about $4,000, this version equipped with a bench that would fold to become a queen-sized bed, and sporting the likes of a classic tube television mounted up and behind the passenger and driver's seat. Another, stripped-down version from a private seller rested at $1500.00, but it lacked some of the baseline features. I did further research and discovered that the GMC vans from that era were known for having expensive chassis repairs, an added risk when considering how much I would be driving the thing. Yet again I felt disarmed by the moment. A vehicle that could ably serve my needs without having major health or consumption issues did not appear to exist, at least not in the realm of men. It seemed like I was stuck with a minivan or the K.O. bust, but not done by an attractive character. I was caught in the swell.

Until I read about the Honda Element. This boxy, nerdtastic goober was produced for a brief period from 2002-2011, and marketed towards outdoor and recreational activities. At first glance, the vehicle seems like another variation on the widespread KIA Soul, Ford Flex, Scion xB, and Nissan Cube models which burst onto the lot in the early to mid-2000s. It is compact in design, featuring only two primary doors along with "suicide hatches" that open once the front versions have been activated. The streamlined siding offers little suggestion of some internal magic, perhaps in part due to the privacy glass that wraps around the back end.

My initial thought was, *This thing is a bizarre clunker!*, so I did not proceed with high hopes.

As it turns out, the Element is one of the strongest contenders for vehicle living outside of a larger van or RV. Where I was looking to have space, the car delivered. With a mostly unassuming appearance, it also scored well. Finally, the fuel economy wasn't insanely crappy like most large SUVs.

Once you get past the eccentric, plastic-and-paint exterior and open the doors, the Honda Element reveals a fascinating ingenuity which caters to multiple possibilities. The central point surrounds the back row of seats. Unlike a typical SUV, where they are bolted to the floor of the car, these ones operate on a hinge system which is locked into the internal siding. A quick disconnect of the floor piece allows you to swing the seats up and alongside the side windows, where a heavy-duty strap with carabiner clip secures around the safety rail grips. What remains is the design of a much-expanded cargo area where you can live, sleep, and make nocturnal merriment (take that as you will). For myself, this provided the liberty to roll out a mat and air mattress behind the front seat (after sliding it forward), along with my sleeping bag. I now had a snug little bed that miraculously fit me, despite my inconvenient height of 6'2".

Because I chose to sleep on the vehicle's floor, the Element's design permitted me to fold the seat up at night, and lower it back down when I was prepared to drive, so as to not impair vision. It is entirely possible to drive the car safely with one or both seats folded up, however. My earlier experiences sleeping in a vehicle were not very uplifting given the misery of trying to recline on a sedan chair, but I swiftly found the resting area to be gentle and comforting, with one of those obnoxiously soft MyPillow cushions thrown in for good measure. In case you're wondering, I got it used, NOT off of the television set for a couple of convenient payments.

On the opposite side I elected to keep the seat locked in place with a plastic storage cabinet planted in the leg area right ahead of it. Here I would store my wardrobe of clothing, along with whatever valuables I decided to not be clasping close to my historic treasures at night. The base of the seat made a nice area to place folded pairs of pants and a laundry tote over them where used clothes could congregate happily, freeing other areas from the delicious stench. Behind the seat I located a set of storage bags, one refrigerated for perishables and the other a depot I would use to store dry items, such as rice and paper towels.

Another nifty benefit of the Element relates to the location of the sunroof. If you have a rack of some sort on top, it is possible to mount a solar panel on the roof which can be run through the sliding gap to power your laptop or other electronic device. Mobile power severely reduces the inconvenience of vehicle living, so it's a good option to try.

3. The Nitty-Gritty of Vehicle Living

1. Startup Costs

It is common to reference vehicle living as a good avenue to shrink personal expenses on the grandest scale. I was especially motivated to achieve this goal through my experiment, so I resolved to maximize value in the various components being purchased instead of blowing large amounts all at once. Whether you plan to or not, living in a car will cause you to drift in the direction of minimalism, if only for reasons of sheer practicality. Under the minimalist approach, you concentrate spending in the direction of items and products that serve basic, everyday needs, without necessarily having luxury purposes. You will likely possess limited space to operate in the confines of the vehicle to begin with, making the hoarder mentality even less appealing.

In point, I focused my sights on snagging a used Element that I could buy outright, evading any sort of debt enslavement plan. Dealers in the surrounding area proved unhelpful, so I made a risky bet on someone's private Craigslist sale. Mine was a 2004 with reasonable mileage listed at $5100.00, which I knocked down to $4900.00 for the purchase price. Elements can range widely in price when they are used, but I was content with the model, which only required a few minor repairs to be in prime working condition. That being said, I advise going through a dealer if possible due to the warranty factor.

To simplify the remaining sections, I chose to insert the following table and provide a sense of how much I was spending by employing the van life model. This is crucial because a lot of folks will treat it like some weird fad, spending tens of thousands to meet the expectations of the dubya dubya web, even if it makes no sense financially. You should be shooting for somewhere between 3-7k at the launch, depending on what the vehicle market is like and whether you live in a really cold place.

Item	Cost Basis	Source
2004 Honda Element	$4900 +$200 (Title Fee) less $3000 (trade-in of my sedan) = $2100.	Craigslist
Car Repairs	Alternator ($600), plus Ignition Switch ($55).	Mechanic Shop/Amazon

WolfTraders -30° Sleeping Bag	$129.99	Walmart	
AceMining Personal Fan	$17.99	Amazon	
Wellax Sleeping Pad	$29.99	eBay	
Blavor Solar Charge Bank	$28.99	Amazon	**Total Startup Costs:** **$2,963 (rounded)**

2. Bagging Some Sleep

Next, I looked into buying a sleeping bag that could accommodate the diverse contours of my living conditions. Taking into account my previous experience with camping, I knew that going too cheap with a bag meant paying down the road due to quality issues. I was determined to get something that would keep me cool and dry, regardless of how hot or freezing it might be. The latter was perhaps more important; letting yourself go cold can lead to issues with hypothermia, which is either damaging or fatal. This should lead you to stay away from everyday stocked department store brands such as Ozark Trail; they might be great on a nice spring or summer night when you want to play with your girlfriend in a truck bed, but are poor options when the weather turns itself over to the sharp BDSM of Captain Cold.

Another issue is how limited quality will reflect on the zippers. Having the zipper break and turn your bag into a blanket is not going to help, particularly on chillier days in the urban wild. A sleeping bag functions properly by "holding in" the heat, not as an open deckchair for Jack Frost.

My choice deliberately strove to not align with this mournful narrative. I initially stumbled across a model rated to no less than -40 degrees Fahrenheit, an insane figure. This lovely piece retailed at $800.00, which swiftly pushed it out of the workability scale for minimalism. The following option was much better. While browsing for cold weather gear on Opera I discovered a Walmart.com special called the WolfTraders -30 degree bag, with a $129.99 price tag. I was a bit apprehensive due to buyers being responsible for return shipping in the event of a bad fit, but I decided to take the risk and made a purchase.

The bag turned out to be nothing short of amazing in action. Like most regular bags, it sports a plasticized coating on the exterior, but that's where the similarities die. Inside the lining is a reinforced polyester and wool material which leaves you generously shielded from the reality surrounding. When I got into it the bag was so effective that I literally could not feel exterior temperatures apart from the extents of my skull that occasionally ventured out at the top. Its enhanced rectangular shape means a far roomier pouch than normal, and the zipper is a large, heavy-duty type which voids the constant problem of blanket sheet bags mentioned earlier. All my experiences sleeping inside were positive from the standpoint of temperature, so it was well worth the purchase. For warmer months, you can switch to a lighter bag, or simply employ a blanket to avoid the sweat-mongering conditions of a winter sleeping cocoon.

3. Staying Warm

Here I would like to make a critical point: keeping warm when you are resting has as much to do with the bag you're in as the clothes you wear. As a general rule, I would change my socks every 6-8 hours while working. In the event I was going to sleep in my car, I would always remove my shift socks, dry off my feet with a paper towel, and put on a fresh pair. This practice gets sweat off your body, especially in the regions where you lose the most heat. Leaving damp socks on inside shoes seals a bunch of moisture against the skin, which can give you a head cold or, in more extreme situations, hypothermia.

Make sure to consider other vulnerable areas as well. A lot of sweat accumulates in the groin and armpit areas throughout the day. Think about changing into fresh undergarments and shirts before retiring for the day. Another tactic is to boil water at work and fill up a hot water bottle to help support warmth. In addition, you may want to employ some type of hat to counter the exposure of your head at the top of the bag. Some of you may wish to wear a beanie hat for this purpose; I don't like the pressure around the temple myself, so I used a lose-fitting balaclava that provided better room to operate. You should however maintain some sort of opening at the bag's peak, as the alternative is a contained chamber where your cold breath can make you sick. Ventilation and exhaust are good, as long as you handle them correctly.

A final aspect I want to discuss relates to temperature adjustment. Should you elect for a climate controlling bag like the WolfTraders model mentioned, you'll want to carefully regulate how rapidly you transition to the outside after waking up. I would typically remain snugly in the bag while squiggling (for lack of a better term) to the front of the car, where I could start the engine and heater. This method allowed me to first change into the new day's clothes, and then exit the bag at a temperature more conducive to the surrounding environment. Keeping those clothes inside the bag for 10-15 minutes works wonders, particularly on colder days. I learned early on that swiftly moving from the bag to the outside world left me with the sniffles, if not a cold entirely.

4. What Do You Do For Heat?

An obvious (and repeated) question from those looking into van living is the toasty one: How do you generate heat for your supermodel body? It was one of my foremost concerns when I began investigating van life for the cardinal reason that I find it exceptionally difficult to work or enjoy life with a head cold. My eyes become watery glass, they drip and drool all over the place, and time seems to stop moving. Since it is easy to get infected from poor temperature control, I wanted maximum protection before taking the step.

My first (abortive) attempt to address this problem involved purchasing the 3800-BTU Mr. Heater, a popular propane-fueled option that retails in department stores for between 60-70 bucks. The machine is designed almost like a lighthouse, with a base to rest the fuel can and a screw-in turret that emits heat. It supposedly lasts for up to six hours at max performance (and without the blue pill). According to the designers, the flame will shut off in case it tips over to prevent a large-scale fire.

From the start, I encountered problems with using propane heat. You deal with the immediate issues of locating the device safely. In my

Element, bountiful space was already taken up due to the other components, leaving the only level position towards the back, right next to my cooler bag. This meant my sleeping bag head or tail (depending on which I chose) being right next to the flame if I elected to keep it on during the night. Because propane can also create toxic fumes, a window had to be kept open for exhaust, which had the marked effect of lowering internal temperature substantially, and undercutting the machine's usefulness. Limited space also proved problematic when I considered carrying propane cans with me. Not only is there an explosive hazard; the number needed would occupy valuable living quarters in my compact vehicle. I also stood to add another monthly expense by having to purchase the cans, which normally run about $3.50 for one, or $6.40 for a pair. After testing the heater for a few weeks, I returned it to the store for a refund.

With the heating problem being significant, especially in colder states, there are a few possible options which can serve as alternatives. For one, get the proper sleeping bag and wear fresh thermal socks and gloves when you sleep. Getting a second bag to add layers or a battery-powered blanket can further reinforce your comfort level when the temperature drops. Unless you are working inside your vehicle, the heat issue is only a major one when you sleep with the car's heater switched off. A healthy possibility in this situation involves people who work overnight. You can rig a solar panel through the moon roof, as mentioned earlier, and use this setup to power a small personal heater such as the Lasko MyHeat 100-200W model. Assuming a decent provision of sunlight, you should have no problem generating enough power to claim a reasonable internal temperature.

An additional method I employed to combat the cold was to purchase a good supply of the hand warmers sold in retail shops and keep them in my vehicle. These pockets are cheap in bulk and can provide warmth without the fire or battery death hazards presented by other routes. They will not project heat into a car's interior very well, but tossing some in the bottom of your sleeping bag makes a huge difference for the comfort index. You can even get gloves that sport a pouch behind the knuckles where these rascals can be stored in the name of closer contact. There are also companies in the business of selling shirts and socks with battery packs that generate reasonable heat. I personally have used the Volt shirt and socks to decent effect, although the wiring system is fragile and prone to easy tearing.

5. Sweating Time

We've dealt with the chills, but what happens when the sun goes all smother smack down on your poor, innocent soul? This issue will vary depending on what part of the country you are in, but I found the solution to have two parts: location and circulation. At the outset, you need to choose carefully when it comes to where you park, especially if you will be waking around or after sunrise. Pay attention in particular to where the sun will rise, sit at midday, and set. There were times when I parked in a specific spot of the lot where there appeared to be some kind of shade or shadow cover, but the shifting of the sun's beams caused me to awake in a mobile sauna, which was rough. Even with the dark privacy glass surrounding the back of my Element, I was getting pierced by the rays in a steamy and highly uncomfortable manner. If you can, find a spot in the parking lot situated against a tree line and facing where the sun rises; depending on the location, it should keep you out of the sun's way regardless of the time of day. Quick note: parking lot or parking garage lights can be similarly obnoxious, so choose carefully such that you don't have gushing LEDs in your eyes when you attempt to snooze.

On the second point, you'll want to incorporate both screens and a circulation system. You can buy a set of window filters or baby sunscreens with the suction mounts for a relatively small price. These will reduce the internal temperature and delimit annoying flashes from the sun. You should also invest in one or more battery-operated fans to keep air moving throughout the vehicle. I personally have used the AceMining model off of Amazon, which is fairly reliable, although its blue power light is obnoxious when you're trying to sleep. I also employed one of the basic Holmes fans to provide extra airflow. The climate you're in may well dictate the need for more fans, so that becomes an individual choice. For myself, having a cool flow of air across my face on a hot night was more than enough to get those logs sawed. And of course you should at least crack your windows to ensure things don't get too stuffy.

6. Mattress Love

Yeah, sorry to disappoint: this mainly concerns buying a mattress. When I started out, I had used an old somersault mat as the base for sleeping, but this proved to be immensely uncomfortable, especially in the event I turned on my side at night, so something else was needed. You can certainly go in different directions with this category; some elect for pricy memory foam mattresses, while others stick with the simpler camping gear. In my case, I found an inflatable camping mat on Amazon which fit my needs well. The retail price was $39.99, but I did some snooping and picked it up on eBay for ten bucks less. The Wellax Sleeping Pad functions simply enough: you manually inflate it with your sexy breath, and the raised bubble pattern works to absorb different contours of body position in the name of comfort. Despite my height of 6'2, I could readily use the pad without risking substantial unpleasantness, as the design does well to accommodate even larger frames. I chose to lay the mat on top of the somersault model to provide extra support, and the result was a reasonably gentle experience while sleeping. It obviously will not be on the same level of luxury as a normal spring and mattress bed, but I typically slept soundly for 6-8 hours in my vehicle each night, so it comes down to the individual.

As far as air retention is concerned, I never found myself having to inflate the little bastard more once every few weeks, and this was usually because I would accidentally kick open the air seal. Whenever you find it necessary to fill up once more, about 5-6 human gusts will do the trick. My model also came with a patching kit that is usable in the event a tear occurs.

7.   Power and Generation

In a world where technological devices have become almost second nature in our everyday lives, having a power source is critical. Some people can handle this problem by charging their phone at work or using a library, yet these options are only viable if you have access to the building, which might be difficult depending on your schedule. Being able to generate power on the go thus becomes essential, but the question remains, how? I previously detailed how you can run a solar panel line through the sunroof and charge devices off of that supply. In my case, I could do all critical functions on my smartphone (an LG Harmony), so the need for such a tremendous power source was noticeably diminished. Instead, I opted to purchase a smaller solar power bank from Amazon called the Blavor, which is rated to 10,000 mAh. This neat little device sports several different inputs for charging lines, along with a dual flashlight and weather resistant coating. I could simply lay the pack on my dashboard and run a cable back to the armrest compartment, where my phone stayed out of sight and plugged in. The result was a snappy charge time that helped keep my phone in healthy battery range while I labored.

I learned later on of a downside to this model, however. After a month and a half the unit stopped charging effectively off of the sun, leaving me with a brick that would accumulate at best 5-10 percent worth of juice before conking out. The customer service representatives claimed the device required 56 hours of direct sunlight to charge, which is pretty ridiculous when you consider how little strong sunshine we get during most days of the year. I got a refund and elected to use the Blavor as a portable phone battery, yet the superior charge time of a wall outlet remanded it to limited use. Based on my experience I would advise simply buying a couple high quality phone battery packs and foregoing the smaller solar models.

8. Refrigeration

Obviously, a regular vehicle is not going to have a built-in fridge, at least not in most cases. At the same time, this does not mean you are without ways of keeping perishables alive and content. When I began the experiment it was during the colder months, so I settled for one of those insulated zip cooler bags used by folks who are trying to transport frozen goods safely from the store to their table without being left with a soupy soufflé. This functioned properly enough, allowing me the storage space to accommodate my regular diet of fruits, vegetables, yogurt, and meat. Because my worksite has a refrigerator of its own, I could easily transfer the especially vulnerable food stuffs to a permanent location, pretty much eradicating the possibility of them going bad. As the warmer months approached, I decided to go with the Titan model cooler, which you can snag at Costco for under twenty bucks. This goober has the normal outdoor wrapped material, and an interior plastic tub for storage. I figured when the car's inside heated up during the summer, added protection would hardly be a bad thing. The best part about this side of the debate is that you can easily find a decent cooler bag secondhand, rendering the price point almost negligible. Just make sure it doesn't come with secondhand food as well.

A wise approach to summertime cooling is to buy a couple of reusable ice packs (or make your own by tossing cubes in multiple layers of Ziploc bags). You can go ahead and refreeze them during working hours in the office fridge, and then pop them back in the trunk for regular use. Providing that your cooler is of decent quality, the food should remain at a crisp temperature during transport.

9. **Internet Access**

Like with phones, internet usage is pretty much a daily activity for most folks, so keeping an open line remains important. At the simplest level, you might only be using a smartphone for everyday browsing. In my case this would be Cricket on a prepaid basis, but various options abound depending on what part of the nation you are occupying. The specific plan you choose will either foster data limits or offer essentially unlimited coverage. If it's the latter, access might not be much of a problem. For myself, I use mobile data sparingly to begin with, so I only signed up for 5GB a month. This is a number I seldom ever break, but you can easily stretch your figures by utilizing free Wi-Fi zones. Cafes are an option, but my preference is the public library; it is usually much quieter, less disruptive, and at least in my experience the signal quality remains superior. Staying out of cafes also maximizes the likelihood that you avoid spending money on high end coffee and scones, which add up at the end of the year.

I must note that I'm astonished by how many folks seem totally unaware of the availability of the library as a resource; you are paying taxes to support the institution, but simply allowing others the privilege of using it. Unless your library system is poorly-stocked or under-funded, there are plenty of other benefits. Today, a strong library branch will give you access to books, music, movies, video games, audiobooks, and even online streaming. Our goal with vehicle living is to save money, so these options beat sending in Amazon orders around the clock for entertainment purposes.

Should the prospect of relying on public Wi-Fi be unappealing to you, there's also the possibility of snagging a mobile hotspot to keep in your vehicle. A Verizon Jetpack model starts at $200.00 for the unit and $30.00 per month for 4GB. You can elect to jack yourself up to 100GB, but that raises the price majorly, which might stray outside the reduced cost living range. The upside is having access to steady wireless internet even if a central hub is not right next door. I am not certain how well they function in rural areas, but those who I have talked to seem to be fairly satisfied with the results.

10. Crapping and Washing

It has been said many times before that these two basic actions are critical to any effective economy, ecosystem, or committed relationship. You certainly have to go, whether in civilized facilities or some kind of portable bladder. Whether you like it or not, the die has been cast in your name. On the other hand, washing may seem like a nonessential employee to some homo sapiens, but it certainly falls under the not-so-liberal leave category. Try going without a bath or at least some valiant deodorant protein shake routine for a few days. Unless you're perpetually in a state of love-making on the Cinemax channel, the soaked sweat and dirt is liable to swiftly alert people to your presence – and cause them to keep a safe distance. The lovers will be losing.

Remarkably, even folks with ready access to facilities at their homes manage to procrastinate on the matter, and yet it's one that a van dweller should be especially cautious with. You will sweat inside a sleeping bag and car, most notably during the summer, but in colder months this will happen as well. The cemented odor, and even more so the general feeling that you are "wearing dirt" will be reason enough to exercise extreme caution.

As far as where you can go about finding access to the scented basics, it becomes a matter of circumstance. For myself, there was a reasonably-sized gym with bathrooms and showers available at my place of work, so an external location proved unnecessary. Nonetheless, I went ahead and performed research into other possibilities at 24-hour gyms. You are going to want a facility open around the clock for fairly obvious reasons. If you happen to experience a 3AM German shelling attack, you'll definitely need a safe location to discharge. In addition, it allows you to safely align your schedule to quieter hours. Those of you who frequent gym facilities during peak times know how obnoxious it can be, particularly if the facility is on the smaller side. The following is a list of popular gym chains that fall in the 24-hour range:

- Anytime Fitness

- Planet Fitness (not really a gym but hey)

- LA Fitness

- 24 Hour Fitness

- Snap Fitness

- Crunch Fitness

Make sure you use caution when it comes to gym memberships; a lot of them are so desperate for revenue that they will try to drag you in with a sexy monthly rate while avoiding to add in the hidden charges until things are long past too late. They are also wary about offering free passes. One of the companies listed above tried to snooker me into a monthly payment plan simply to try them out for a day. When I balked at this, they pushed a pricy charge for use on a one-time basis. I fully appreciate how these companies are trying to crackdown on freeloading, but at the same time, cost reduction is central to vehicle living.

Also, verify whether the facility is large enough to justify your membership costs. The last thing you want is a value meal spot where you must do battle for access to a shower or your preferred gym equipment. Even in the case of larger brands the individual locations may be independently-owned, resulting in disparate size provisions and equipment selection. These are the places you walk in and walk out, because nothing worthwhile is available to use.

11. Laundry Time

Unless you're one of the lucky few who doesn't sweat or reek, you're going to need a way to replenish fresh clothes on a consistent basis. Much as you might have learned in college to go Febreze Tactical in order to save money (or merely time) and not have to wash your clothes, the working world isn't friendly to this method. You will start to smell, and if that's not bad enough at work, where you are making an ill-advised play for the blonde with the XL booty stuffed into an XS skirt, it will pose a problem in the car. Foul-smelling fabrics DO conspire to make your life unpleasant, particularly if you are trying to sleep during the winter without every window peeled down for circulation.

There are a couple ways to handle this problem in a manner mutually beneficial to yourself and those around you. To begin, you could simply use a laundromat. They are widely available and relatively inexpensive, although you must be agreeable to the idea of hanging out in such an environment for an extended period of time. Speaking as someone who saw an armed robbery in progress as my clothes were slowly flipping about in the dryer, I can vouch for the funkiness. You should also keep in mind how the location is arranged. I have experienced laundromats where you could wash your clothes in one cycle, but the dryers only allowed 7-minute increments for their loops, so you ended up wasting lots of time trying to reach a "not damp" status for the fabric. And the chubby Crips member staring at you with a perplexed look half the time? More fun for the ride.

The primary alternative possibility is to pay someone you know for weekly usage. I opted for this route because I was not pleased with the waiting time at my local laundromat, and I felt uneasy about leaving my things out in the public fray. It might seem odd as a message from someone willing to sleep in their car, but I am extraordinarily vigilant when it comes to preventing myself from being robbed. I have had it happen before, and usually due to carelessness. If you have a hookup that will let you employ their machines for one or two cycles a week, go ahead and pursue the option. Just make certain they are getting paid, and be courteous. If you are doing a small load of laundry, don't use the large water option; regardless of what you might have been told, more is not always a good (or necessary) thing. Vehicle living is ultimately about minimalism, so there should be no exceptions here. Of course you can always give your clothes a good scrubbing at the local stream or river, but after that they may or may not come alive.

12. Where You Can Park

When folks approach van life, there can a tendency to not properly consider stable living requirements. For instance, some eager lemonheads will examine the possibility of simply buying a small plot of land and parking a camper or RV on top of it. This sounds like a great way to beat the system, but like with other bold proposals to protect your wallet, good old Aunt Samantha is standing by to spank that naïve upstart before they can sing. The short of it is, you can't, or at least not without much subterfuge. States and localities almost universally deem a dwelling on wheels to be a recreational vehicle, which means you are prohibited from treating it like a normal residence on property you own. Yes, the concept bewilders every "This is America," argument, but it stands nonetheless. Going against such statutes might work in an obscure or isolated zone, but all it takes is a snoopy neighbor to put in the call, and you're looking at substantial fines. The same is true of trailers or tiny homes. If you're trying to go small to save money, be prepared to shell out cash to construct a foundation.

The tenacious peppercorns among you will naturally point to RV parks as an alternative. After all, camping cannot possibly be the same price as renting, especially seeing that you are stuck outdoors and exposed to the eyes of the night. The problem is that such spots can actually be worse than a basic studio department, depending on the region you're located in. Some of the rates I found at local sites were in the mid-forties range PER NIGHT. That comes to a rather lofty $1200.00 each month, which is more than a cheap apartment will run you. Further exacerbating the issue is site policies on long-term camping. Certain locations will close during colder seasons, or simply prohibit you from hanging out past the thirty day mark at any one time. Things might have been different in the past, but as housing costs soar our friends in the real estate system find outlets to make money anywhere possible.

The critical aspect to appreciate when it comes to van living is that you will not be able to rely on stationary positions for extended periods of parking. Moving about is a good idea in general, as you avoid becoming too much of a regular and attracting the attention of neighborhood patrols, or even law enforcement. Some solid locations to employ include the following:

- Department stores

- Gas stations

- Rest stops

Be sure to use measured caution with all of these options. First, consider the size of the parking lot, and the level of lighting. Pulling into the far corner of a big department store lot isn't going to be a huge issue, but occupying space at some compact 7-11 might be troublesome. Make certain the area is lit up properly; you might not be Public Enemy No. 1 as a mobile person, but there's always the possibility of a moron high on crack paying you a visit. In line with this threat, know your area. Police reports are publicly available, with some municipalities offering digital crime maps for further reference. Such info can help you avoid parking in the ratchet section of town where even cops are afraid to tread.

Go ahead and make a list (or GPS map point group) outlining the various spots you intend to use. By categorizing them and using a rotating schedule, you can ensure there is no lingering question once you are tired and ready to bed down. You might even put the data into a spreadsheet and jumble it to certify that you are never at the same place on the same day regularly. Perhaps it seems over-the-top, but in today's world being loose with security is not the best choice. At bare minimum, you avoid developing a pattern which bystanders could take note of if they wish to target you.

13. The Watchful Neighbor Factor

"There's always some prick." This roughly summarizes my experience with the public in the course of going about the van living process. To be clear, most people aren't going to care one way or the other; they might glance momentarily at the sight of someone packing a vehicle with an obvious and visible sleeping area, but that's about the extent to which it goes. At best they're liable to be thinking "Better you than me," or "Who WOULDN'T' want to pay $1900.00 monthly for rent?" Docile indifference will be their standard operating procedure.

What I'm actually referring to is the way you will likely feel about your surroundings while living in a vehicle. In my case, I had limited room to work due to the compact nature of the Element, so I consistently felt the need to be wary of people in the vicinity of a parking lot if I was changing or doing some work in the car. Not only will you have curious folks who stray their eyes while passing by in the most bizarre fashion; some people actually like to sit in their own vehicle and simply observe – both you and others nearby. These are not cops – least not in my case – but rather bored and nosy people with little else to do for entertainment.

My biggest piece of advice in this regard is to have the right vehicle and simply focus on whatever your immediate task is. With my Element I could draw up the seats alongside the privacy glass windows, leaving minimal hints as to what was happening inside. My sleeping bag's expanded dimensions also proved helpful in providing cover for changing, albeit with a dose of clumsiness. If you're lucky enough to have a classic camper van, you can easily sport some curtains at the front and leave yourself with immense privacy against the world around.

Regardless of the size, you have to adapt to the reality of enjoying less space and privacy. There is no longer a full bedroom and bathroom available just several steps away. The vehicle model is the space you have, with perhaps a few potential modifications. You will have to flexible when it comes to your comfort demands, and try hard to blot out the wandering

eyes from angry local fishmongers that seem to drift your way.

14. More On Privacy

This topic is well worth devoting a separate block to because it

remains an almost universal imperative for different folks. Individually, I

am an immensely private person. I don't have an issue with socializing or

enjoying the company of others, but I need a certain measure of solitude to

refresh and revamp my energies. Constant contact gets to be obnoxious

after a time, and thus I like to withdraw slightly. While it might not seem

that way in passing, even extroverted people have the same problem: they

don't like to experience overload. As humans we often require some

separation, if not for any other reason than to think and remind ourselves

that we exist as individuals, not simply as part of a thundering blob.

With this in mind, the endeavor of car living might seem a tad

insane to those looking to maintain their personal privacy, but it doesn't

have to be. You just need to learn how mental organization works.

Previously, your sanctum might have been your room (or living room)

depending on the type of abode. For some people it is (at maximum

cringe) their bathroom. When we get to the topic of a car, the key is to treat

it like your new sanctuary. It is the place you retreat, with reasonable

security, to detox from the intensity and fury of the world (assuming your

life is that interesting). This is where vehicle choice becomes a prized virtue. Some folks will buy a house in a specific area because it happens to be more secluded. The simple decision to pick a home over a studio apartment might meet the same end: you really want to be away from others, at least part of the time. If your car choice falls into the sedan category, this becomes exceptionally difficult to tackle. The principal setup already restricts movement, and trying to "live" amid the quarters results in little action beyond the driver's seat. That being said, action in the front seat isn't always a bad thing. Just choose the right vehicle.

15. Loneliness

Probably the least-examined topic where vehicle living is concerned would be how you go about dealing with a LACK of human contact. It's a more critical issue than most people wish to admit. We follow distinct patterns of social conglomeration in life, starting from a ripe young age. We live with our families, roommates or significant others, and, for the exceptionally brave, spouses and children. Some folks have no problem inhabiting spaces alone, but for others, regular human contact is essential to them functioning in a halfway normal manner. Even if you happen to be less outgoing as a person, chances are socialization fits into some part of your life, big or small. For this reason, the realization of what it takes to live out of your car can feel daunting, particularly if you're used to being around lots of people.

In my experience, there is a very effective way to counteract the problem which also works towards the goal of building social confidence. Living out of your car obviously sets you apart from the regularity native to interacting with co-inhabitants or a spouse (if you still talk), but by no means does it have to be pledged completely to some realm bereft all socialization. The main advantage of the lifestyle is in the way it MOTIVATES you to pursue that socialization, both at work and in your free time. I have always looked for opportunities to practice conversation with co-workers or customers during the course of my work hours because it is free, and often entertaining. Few things can make a long shift go by faster than good, or hilarious, discussion. Beyond that, you can use your position in the life model to forge new relationships with those you don't know. As a matter of tradition, I always try to engage with people while I am out and about. This could be the grocery store cashier, another customer at the gas station, or a librarian. Most people are willing to talk, especially if you ask questions specifically pertaining to them as individuals. This is especially true with women. The very fact that you ask the question or make an observation is a demonstration of interest, which proves compelling in the hearts of the typical human bean. It does not need to be terribly elaborate, either. A basic lead might be asking about the status of business, complimenting their shoes, or even figuring out what they like doing outside of work. I've made a considerable number of friends using this particular foundation. You have to consider that most people don't go out of their way to converse with anyone in a setting that is outside the prototypical "social" sphere, such as a bar or club. At minimum, you are placing yourself in a category unique to the world, and thus maximizing the likelihood that they notice or remember who YOU are. Even if you don't intend to pursue van life, I would recommend trying it out sometime. You'll likely be amazed at how receptive folks become once they realize you are interested in their own lives.

16. How Much I Saved

As we established previously, a central component of the van life movement is to allow for the saving of money on unnecessary overhead and regular costs of "existence expenses." These are the charges that you otherwise cannot ignore, lest you find some glorious gender neutral sugar provider to pay for them. It's not a question of cutting back or shrinking them; you have to pay based on your lifestyle. In my case, living in my vehicle allowed me to slash with more fervor than Paul Ryan in a lucid congressional dream. To start, I eliminated most of my previously regular gas expenses. When I was commuting with my sedan, I would fill up 2-3 times a week, depending on whether I had something going on over the weekend. The average of these charges came in around $50.00, whereas van life brought it to an average of $30.00 weekly. A quick tabulation of 26 weeks gives us $1300 under the previous model minus $780.00 on the newer version, with a savings of $520.00 on gas.

My life of commuting also demanded frequent oil changes, typically around the price of one week's worth of gas ($50.00) every two months, or $150.00 for 26 weeks. With the van life approach I could go 8-9 months on a single oil change, leading to savings of at least $100.00. Furthermore, my lack of intensive driving resulted in minimal automotive issues during my trek, compared to more regular problems when I was putting over 600 miles on the rascally sedan each week.

It is also worth considering the expenses I avoided simply by opting for the vehicle living path. Going by the market rates where I am located, I would have been in for $700.00 monthly plus utilities for simply renting a room (around $4680 over six months). If I insisted on more luxurious accommodations and demanded an apartment of my own, we would have been looking at $1100 monthly plus utilities, or $7080 for the same period. These might seem like chickenfeed to some folks, but any additional money you possess after expenses is a boon when it comes to early retirement, or merely financial security. Due to the van life concept I was able to consistently save \$3-4k monthly, something that would have been impossible under the previous renting and commuting arrangement.

17. Should You Do Van Life?

With all this information in mind, you might be curious as to whether I advocate van life to the world on a large scale. The short answer is a Mel Gibson-style hell no. While I enjoyed the experience and all the freedom it carried, I am well aware of how the Liberal State enjoys subsuming anything that strays even slightly near its perimeter wire through regulation and taxes. Van life as a concept is best reserved for a small community of liberty-minded people searching for ways to cut their costs and relish the simplicities of life. If it manages to catch on as some sort of fad, I fear the original principles will be lost amid another revenue extraction bonanza.

In regards to your relative compatibility with van life, it will come down to individual background and willingness to adapt. I would not advise embarking on the adventure if you have an impeccable love for comfort, Central Air, and social acceptability. A vehicle abode means being at the mercy of the local elements (haha), which could entail waking up with the sniffles when it is chilly, or being caked with Young Spice sweat oil during the summer's underbelly period. It might involve holding in your Gatorade until the next morning because you don't have a toilet handy (although you could use a bottle). Above all, you can expect your friends to view you with cocked chances and bewilderment over the one bedroom studio on wheels.

For the folks who can shrug it off and proceed, focused on their life and personal interests, these downsides are but chatter in the wind. In the case of others (probably the supermajority), the price is too steep to pay. I respect either group, but realism is important. Do not invest thousands of dollars into a vehicle you will not use simply because the niche trend catches your eye; you have to be honest with yourself about whether you can deal with the gnarly parts just as much as the glitzy, internet side. At the end of the day, an overpriced apartment or your parents' basement is better than utter misery because the wheels don't tickle your fancy.

4. Conclusion : What It Taught Me

I must admit, it is odd to conceive of the experience living in a vehicle as a vessel to explore one's understanding of themselves and the world around. A car is after all just a means of transportation, and the humble interior with its scratches and torn seats doesn't magically convey the designs of some mystical realm. Several bits of metal and plastic, assembled along a line on the other side of the world, powered by the welcome touch of a gas-slurping motor – is this the recipe list for personal reflection and understanding?

Remarkably, the answer is yes. What I stepped away from at the end of my humble sojourn was an experience that forced me to understand myself, and how far I could withdraw from the normal traditions of life. Many folks remember the story of *Walden* by Henry David Thoreau, a brilliant saga about a man who disconnects from society to live in a cabin alone. My Element was likewise a distinct world operating on its own terms. Behind the interlocking doors I had to embrace the simplicity of a life without formality, without extravagance, and absent waste. I could no longer expect to lounge aimlessly in bed, half awake and partly gone, because my room lay exposed to the rattling noises around. I was forced to be bolder, to eliminate time trenches consumed by rudderless thought, and to make do with less than before. Prior to the leap, I would go through multiple tanks of gas commuting across the sprawl of a regular week; with van life I stretched the precious resource to further lengths. I also downsized my wardrobe, keeping only what I needed and eliminating excess clutter that had commanded much space where I rented. Perhaps more importantly, I was able to survive the constant anvil of social pressure which is foisted on young people so they conform to public expectations about lifestyle. Ultimately, I thought little of how others perceived me, and more of what would allow my life to prosper in the way I wanted it to.

The end of text, but the road goes on…

About the Author

Martin Goldberg is a wonderful human bean who has also authored the books *Total Invincibility* and *Ass Culture*. When he's not chuckling at his own handiwork, he can be found working as an amateur gardener and fitness expert. He makes his home in Florida land. You can find him online pretty easily with a web browser search. There are no others like him.

www.ingramcontent.com/pod-product-compliance
Lightning Source LLC
Chambersburg PA
CBHW021513210526
45463CB00002B/999